THE BE

THE BEST PREY

THE BEST PREY
PAIGE QUIÑONES

LENA-MILES WEVER TODD PRIZE SERIES
WARRENSBURG, MISSOURI

ISBN 978-0807175484
Copyright © 2021 by Paige Quiñones
All rights reserved

Published by Pleiades Press

Department of English
University of Central Missouri
Warrensburg, Missouri 64093

Distributed by Louisiana State University Press

Cover Art: Pat Perry

Book design by David Wojciechowski
First Pleiades Printing, 2021

Financial support for this project has been provided by the University of Central Missouri, as well as the Missouri Arts Council, the Missouri Humanities Council. and the Literary Arts Emergency Fund.

CONTENTS

I

3   A Piece of Living Heart
4   Apophenia
6   Luna de Miel
7   Lineage
8   The Weight of a Girl
9   Dueña del Bosque
11 Black Magic Pact
13 Love Poem: Fox
14 Daughters I Haven't Met
15 Ode to Desire
17 Outpatient Visit Summary

II

23 Omens I Choose to Ignore
24 Ode to My Womb
25 La Operación
27 Mastectomy // Mother
28 Venice Beach
30 Tasseography
31 Rotation Sequence
32 Wedding Day: Lake Alice on a Sunday Morning
34 Aguadilla, PR
35 That Which I Consider Untamable
36 View from a Guest House in Calabasas
38 Visiting My Grandparents' Unmarked Graves
39 Outside the Psychiatric Hospital

41	Viability Study
42	Canopy
43	Inside In
44	At the Museum
45	Still Life with Wadded Paper Towels

III

49	Ode to Hysteria + Anhedonia
51	Intricacies
53	Alternate Realities
54	On the Duality Of
55	Bipolar and its Related Disorders
56	Erosion
57	Elegy Ending on the Ocean Floor
58	I Dreamed in Spanish Once
59	Harlot
60	Stage
61	Epithalamium
62	Things to Do in the Belly of a Whale
63	Ode to Loss
64	Wing Covert

Notes

Acknowledgments

I

A PIECE OF LIVING HEART

is almost as pale as the stem
of a wilting tulip. Mine is transparent, thin
as a spider's web sewn from dusty baseboard

to floor, the fisher asleep at his helm,
a sad slackness to his trap. I watch
as a bee stumbles through, disturbed

by the human audience to his lateness—
the sun swims past the windowsill.
His dull wings catch and the struggle

is slow and some hive is none the wiser
to its loss. But imagine, pretend he is you:
beauty is the cold bind, beauty is the fang,
       I am complicit.

APOPHENIA

I once tried to read the palm of a man I did not know. His fingers were long and could not stay up; he reached for my breast instead. I felt no warmth in his hand or in my chest. All we left was an indentation on the couch, its loose cover twisting, some woman's white veil.

*

I was taught to never look a man in the mouth; rather, I have learned to demand family secrets. I am old enough to know what these mean. I can use them to build a shrine. His father's mistress had long black curls. No words exist for his mother's lovers.

*

Black underwear makes a constellation around my ankles. Capricornus. Backlit by the television, he tells me I resemble a woman. He resembles something else. I run my tongue over the flattest parts of his teeth.

I can feel where he's begun to grow antlers.

*

We watch one another as if the moon does not exist, as if there is body of water between us. I see a man at the bottom of this lake. He sees a doe instead.

*

He preferred bruised fruit to anything.

*

I want to catch my ankle in the spokes of his bicycle. My mother has a scar there too; its silver shines like a polished bone. She told me how it felt to fall forward, her talus flashing in the sun. I find this romantic. I would reach for his hand and kneel and lick the blood from my own leg.

*

We played by laying coins on each other's eyes. I liked him best that way, smelling of stale metal, eyelids ringed in gray. We played by hunting in the dark. He taught me to identify prints, to gut, to dress. He only smiled with his hands deep inside a warm red cut.

*

In the dream, he is a feral child who does not speak. When I wake, he is a shadow moving across the door.
When I wake, I have no mouth to open.

LUNA DE MIEL

    I half-filled
           a goblet with spring water
& placed it in the cavity

        between our halves of the bed
we never spoke about
       our cold new bedmate

after seven weeks
       the silver tarnished
life congealed inside the cup

       its water turned fen-like
evaporation left timestamps
       a diving bell spider made her home

feasting on fairy shrimp & larvae
       she not only ate them
but her own eggs afterward

       when she died her exoskeleton
grew brown algae
       & sank we were still

newly wed the stagnant cup
       leaked black onto our sheets
& I poured the pond out

LINEAGE

One of my fathers played stickball in Harlem.
This father never got a street-kid nickname.
Another father scared well-dressed ladies into
crossing the street before he crossed their paths.
He's told me it was his boots or his brown skin.
A different father found friends stair-slackened:
addicts from whom a boy couldn't turn his gaze.
One father found god and never loved anyone.
Another father played a dented sax, its keys
rusted pearly green underneath the pads.
#6 had his name called to enlist—
he didn't like that one bit. Another father
kept a baby boy in tow. My favorite
stood before the wild and never came back.

THE WEIGHT OF A GIRL

When I asked him how it felt
to have the weight of a girl on top,
I thought of nine months in,
my ring on a chain, swinging
a tight circle, orbiting girl
gravity: the midwife's interpretation,
how full-moon sexed-up heaviness weighed
less than a boy inside a belly, and much,
much less than a man pressing down.
Were he and I reversed, I would
have breathed in sharp
and then not at all. Not so much
is different during sex. I've got a valley
of shadows, and he wanted to live in it,
or at least stay awhile. Afterward, the blanket
over our heads split open:
the world knifed in; we made
dinner. We moved around one another
un-symbiotically. Fuck
imperative. A child
was the last thing I wanted.

DUEÑA DEL BOSQUE

You think you can return to that place
        where your feral tía
        climbed down from the mountain,

where roads bend without reason,
        blanketed in feathers.
        But that place is now overgrown

with a jungle's blue-green fingers.
        A girl once hunted there,
        her urchin-dark eyes searching.

Rats have taken her place.
        A wild dog once leapt against a spiked fence
        to steal a yellow bird from your hands.

A man once told you
        the species you see are not endemic
        so your ancestors never knew them,

never thatched their roofs
        with that kind of plant.
        But your tía still believes

in their magic: she is tall
        because the blood heaving inside her is violent.
        Your grandmother, whenever she held me,

ella sabía que yo era una diabla.
        You are small because you are meek.
        She knows you shrink

from a man's spitting mouth
> because you fear the animal
> you can become at will.

BLACK MAGIC PACT

the devil is my plaything
   so I'll bring the bacchanalia
  to you

my pussy is a cobra's laughing
maw just grope her
to feel my efficient fangs

I have been torn in half
more than once but I know
a potion that might

   make us whole & all
you have to do is touch me
without fear

     I have felt
a beloved's hands on my throat
& hated it

    I have felt Satan
between my legs & perhaps
  craved him

now he becomes
whatever size I command

don't be afraid when I grow
a dragon's tail or a bouquet
in my snarl these are
    my spells

whether or not you like it

I am the witch
                      at your neck

LOVE POEM: FOX

The dogs sing in the wood
and I marvel at their song.

O caved-in burrow, O stench:
marriage of my betrayal.

To dress myself in woman
would be a finer sport;

a rich man would offer a gloved palm
toward the furl of my unnatural grin.

Here, I damn the mocking trees,
the man on his horse, his gloves.

Love, that you might be the silver
of a stream, the dark of a lake:

my refuge in the hunt. Or,
you might be one to drown me.

DAUGHTERS I HAVEN'T MET

Heaven is a river
                filled with flat stones, girls
lining the bank,
                skipping rocks.
As I pass each girl
                & touch her curls,
I see her future
                unfurled
in my palm:
                first kiss,
missing breasts,
                whiskey breath.
Sons. Some have none.
                They've all got
my June-dark skin
                & mouths that
can't quite close.
                One girl catches
sight of her fate,
                steps further
into the white water,
                & begs me to hold her
under. *Please*, she says.
                Don't let me be born.

ODE TO DESIRE

O perfect engine
you craft me into
my most
        terrible self

with two mouths two
furious gazes

you break the spines of
my favorite books
                & cover
my body with their
        unbound
          poems

I prefer your lights
        dim like a rolling
black wave

I promise to hold
my knees
                to my chest
when it suits you

please bruise my neck
& make it the color
of   strange
                water

you who are
   the written thing
rather than
     its writer

you only open
your eyes when I'm slick-
   skinned & salt-
     licked

but on those nights
   I need you to

make me into
whatever   version
you like best
 & sink it

OUTPATIENT VISIT SUMMARY

an erasure

   I.

birth a partial reason for
intensive unspecified dependence

you were bipolar and
        borderline

a moderate treat

you may have no
additional   use

   II.

currently in self-psychosis

after initial
appropriate planned marriage

insomnia due to infidelity
with no lost sexual interest

a prior history
    of moving elevations

traits of a woman
      worsening

III.

what are emotions
        but self-medication

she did drink
        contradictions

thoughts   cause shame
and   awareness
and   affairs

they are her enemies as needed

IV.

she is beginning to step
outside her history

and view herself rather
than her patterns of mood

V.

medication   an acute
        fundamental concern

please confirm discontinuing
drugs or direct   sunlight

or damp places

VI.

a habit of replacement

a chewing cessation

keep your medicine list confident

VII.

only use your most recent
                                        mouth

II

OMENS I CHOOSE TO IGNORE

Children sit under street signs eating plums, staining
their chins like used Band-Aids.
                                        A corner of the ceiling
falls in though it hasn't rained for weeks. Your books
on the bedroom floor lie shrouded in plaster.

Merlot's persistent silt lines my glass, never in the shape
of anything.
                      The flat silence after
your neighbor's Doberman escapes—we only sleep
when she returns to her chain.

The children who stole from us leave their bitten pits.

I find every green penny glued face-up on the asphalt.

At night you don't understand
a word I say, laughing as I explain how to gut a fish:
                    if it's done quick, you'll see the heart beating.

        And later, when the dog breaks away once more,
we watch as she looks back at us with a smile,
dark head bending at an impossible angle.

ODE TO MY WOMB

Dear unstocked refrigerator,
you decide on curtain patterns:
damask/velvet, maroon/floral.
You were the first interior decorator,
& how could you be anything
but a woman peering out at me
through what blooms in my underwear?
I hate you at your emptiest.
O little fist, you wait between
two poisons, to swell or wrinkle—
shrill pain squeezing around
the breath I can't catch.
Dear woman crossing her legs
in an airport terminal:
who, but you, starts a war?
What kind of artist can you call yourself
until the only time I'll meet you:
through sound, a topographical map,
black & white even when
you're cherry-red. I was still a child
when I learned I could bleed
from no wound. My sisters already knew:
be careful with boys—the hunt is on.
So send me your pearls,
wrap them in scarlet shrouds,
& I will bury them out back. Send them
& I will offer you my lovers.
I have nothing else to give.

LA OPERACIÓN

I will never know my abuela, but I know her eyes.

She dug her mother's shoes out from graying snowbanks, pulled that black-shawled woman from glass.

Fingers, stained with banana leaves, blistered under hard twine.

Men lined up outside her door, dragging hungry wives and children.

One said, *ella es la reina de Spanish Harlem.*

One said, *she's a beggar's filthy palm.*

She never fed them all.

They groped the doorframe and pried the lock, but all she could say was *duerme duerme duerme.*

And she'd dream too, of fawns lying by roads outside the city.

That they leapt toward her, their eyes black or missing; she feared their hooked necks.

I know she woke from this dream with a son in her arms and her womb on a table.

I know she did not ask for this.

And yet: her body, with its dimpled crags, she admired.

She even admired her son, with his roped knuckles, and the daughter who was not her daughter.

But the space between her belly and spine was still empty: a discarded ring.

MASTECTOMY // MOTHER

The day her hair fell out, she fell asleep
in a tub green from dyed Epsom salts.
She never knew I was there—eyelids shut
but moving slightly, gaze shifting in dreams.
I stayed quiet and examined her new absences.
Sunbursts of veins crossed her scalp, flaring

through thin skin and clusters of shoulder freckles.
The barbed scars bisecting her chest looked
like lips. I realized then that she would die in this
body, stripped of what made her a woman
and a mother. I am ashamed of how long I stared.

In a photo I found of her honeymooning,
she stood in a hotel doorway, wearing a pale
peignoir, dark curls framing a smirk.
I imagined my father putting down the camera
and meeting her where she stood, reaching in,
unfastening the silk to consider the lines of her skin.

VENICE BEACH

We once watched a woman in white cast flowers into the sea
one by one, tearing each away from its stem as if it had wronged her.

I imagined her the blowfish I saw as a child. The fish smiled even
as a fisherman tossed it to my feet.

He tried to guess her prayer, white petals pooling around her ankles
like bones anyway.

Our cheeks touched as we waited for sunset. There was no sunset.
We were unlucky: the sky gunmetal.

He hadn't shaved. I felt sorry for believing her a vagrant.

His hand was a fogged mirror. It searched between my thighs.

*

I would like to fuck you on a pew.
I would like to fuck you in an echoing gallery.
I would like to lick your pussy at the end
of this pier. Among the salt.
No one would see us against the sea.

*

And if I had let him—

if we'd taken off our shoes, if I had exposed my skin
to those drenched planks,

if we'd climbed out to the edge of the world, if I'd opened
my body to his mouth—

I would have had to scrawl my name onto a petal and beg
that woman to bury it so far down the sea could never reach in.

TASSEOGRAPHY

You will look up a word & forget it by morning—

A secret door coming unhinged

Last night the white cup split into three pieces

When you meet the wolfhound do not look her in the face—

The bitch mouths   *tie his wrists down*   & I don't see

He has been invading the wrong house for six months

The password for this trapdoor is *fruitless*

Try feeding him another woman's breastmilk—

Desperation became a thing contagious

I know what your fetters are made of & where you keep them—

Lock pins aligning despite disuse

I predict a wasp nest in your mattress by tomorrow—

The cock-purple marks on his chest cannot fade now

I press into his soft teeth & say   *I made you this*

ROTATION SEQUENCE

It was almost enough to dream
the naked mattress into a pasture.
Odor of a fallow spring despite all we did
to the earth. The fence had fallen and anyone
could slip through, so let's say we hid
during winter instead. No music of growing.
In the most selfish months, we could hear the howls
from miles around and kept our windows barred.
I pretended we hoarded enough to last through March,
that we had the foresight to love quickly.
Standing outside while the first snow fell,
you said you felt like a disobedient child.
So we kept to flattened paths, hunting for rabbits.
Still, I woke to the real heat of your bedroom floor—
I pressed each new day to my palm like a splinter.

WEDDING DAY: LAKE ALICE ON A SUNDAY MORNING

Do you take this man?

Alligators speak
in a guttural language—

their songs advertise
impressive erections.

My dress is white,
its hem already dirty,

and my ring isn't quite
slipping over the joint.

I push it past, kiss
the reddening skin.

I can't help but sway
to the lizard tune,

think *this is the sound
I've been hunting for.*

Underneath my dress
lies a horrid, itchy slip:

mesh made of Spanish
moss, wet and slick.

In sickness and in health?

Dammit, Father,
I'm more than ready.

I take it. I take
this man.

AGUADILLA, PR

August 2015

Only men sit at the fountain, eyeing
my sister's legs & my exposed neck
from across the square.
Women on the doorstep of the *ferretería*
ask for money, spit *gringas* at our backs
when we clench our teeth & do not comply.
A shaded couple trades a stamp
of heroin for money—an exchange, palm
against palm, that ends as quickly as it begins:
a shy kiss, an oar dipping into water.
There are no children here.
We were children here once.
We still photograph the ocean sunset
and pocket the brightest intact shells,
as if this is the place we remember.

      Streets are now lined with empty homes;
      every ceiling, caved & rotting,
      is webbed with nests & vines.
      The sea will make her way inside.

THAT WHICH I CONSIDER UNTAMABLE

There is an animal behind my house. I can smell him from my bedroom. At night, he pulls at the cellar, claws shapes into trees with scores so deep they pulse. An X, an eye, a goat. Mornings, there are birds in neat rows on my doorstep. Starlings, meadowlarks: each breast splayed open like a gentleman's waiting hand. I can only imagine his mouth, that primitive hole, lined in feathers as if *Hope* were a word he could craft. I see him sometimes at the bottom of my stairs, spine low, darkness slinking closer. I light more lanterns. I caught him once, coming away with only a fistful of black and silver fur. Though I keep this tuft in a jewelry box, it is not enough. I would like his entire pelt. I would like to lie in it.

VIEW FROM A GUEST HOUSE IN CALABASAS

This is the most expensive I've ever felt

sitting topless at the edge of the pool,

remembering summers I've wasted

on men like you. I don't understand Los Angeles

with its bloated homes in the valley.

Sometimes I can't tell the difference

between panic and want, between six months

and a single morning. You're sure it won't be long

before this entire coast breaks into the sea but I think

I could stay. Later, someone will tell me to leave a man

if secrecy is the only thing binding us. You are not my husband.

Landscapers wield whirring tools near joggers.

Hummingbirds buzz at bright feeders.

The water is too cold, but I challenge you

to see who can stay under the longest. I'm prepared to lose.

I just want to hold you down on my way up.

VISITING MY GRANDPARENTS' UNMARKED GRAVES

Row after row, this white square
gapes like others; name plates turned

scrap bronze, turned drug money.
Metal remains on few,

blank but for jewel-colored
synthetic petals the wind has carried

from wealthier dead. The grass inside
bears no name, is a woman

without a womb: *hueca*.
The lucky man to the right served in Korea.

Un Padre Querido, his marker tells me.
The grave to the left might well hold

an entire family, or no one; its square,
its grass, its flat expanse is the same

as the one I stand before.
I pray for the contents of both:

the unknown, my abuela buried first,
the man my father calls father.

But my words cannot mark them.
My dead have no use for names.

OUTSIDE THE PSYCHIATRIC HOSPITAL

The patients & I are on a break from group;
the two men smoke Camels & I

need some air. We talk music.
Saw Hendrix in '70, the oldest man says.

He lives alone with his Pomeranian
& is so optimistic in remission

I do not know why he's here.
The HVAC guy tells us about

his garage band: a good hobby
to have. This is small talk.

Back inside, he will insist
I should be happy.

But I am the weakest man I know.
Then: *I think I was raped as a boy.*

It will be the first time I see
a grown man cry, besides my father.

The room will shift its weight,
cross and uncross its legs.

Some people carry a hole
the size of a childhood.

I'm still uncertain I do.
But on this cigarette break,

before we hear him name
that hollow, he touches my shoulder

& says, *I used to write poems too.*
We got that in common.

I bet they were beautiful, I say.

VIABILITY STUDY

a language I wish I never learned

      your off-kilter teeth shone in the mirror

a copy of Barthes, bisected by a black ribbon

      berries held against my nipples for comparison

gold earring exposed in the yard, a year later

      hair floated in a day-old glass of water

an insect's cocoon, yawning, transfigured

      why is it better to last than to burn

CANOPY

The smell of new sap: a woman's voice at the nape of my neck. Making my way into the forest, I'm sure to keep each tree at arm's distance. A skulk of white foxes stands watch and I demand they rearrange into a recognizable shape. But wild animals do not move that way; this is a place of desire. Despite the remoteness, a jet plane overhead. I pretend to set the world on fire. I regret this. Finally, what I've come for emerges: my grandfather's gold watch, hanging from the limb of a balsam fir. It looks as if it's been cleaned by a jeweler. It has never been set in motion.

INSIDE IN

Love is like this, you tell me,

        as you brush a horsefly

off my thigh. We're getting stoned

        and the forest

has approached us

        to say, *last night was nice, but*

I didn't think you'd come back.

        Your hand wasn't fast enough—

a ringed welt, a spot of blood.

        We roll up the car windows to keep

the outside out. *I once watched a deer*

        walk into a convenience store,

I tell you. *Wild animals*

        look weird under fluorescence.

Love is like that.

        Her hooves clicked on the tile,

and she couldn't stand upright.

AT THE MUSEUM

I watch a sparrow circle the glass ceiling
like wool in a spindle. The world was temporary,
now barred from him. He will soon die
of exhaustion. Marble nudes, milky rivers
frozen in the midst of turmoil or eros,
line the atrium. Most people stop
at the occasional statue, speak to their partners,
and do not notice the bird.
A woman with a blank notebook
examines a painting of an abstract man.
I find myself hating it. I ask her
why she carries the notebook and she says
I never remember the paintings. I say the red here
is hard to forget. I think it means blood and warfare.
She tells me *I don't think we're allowed to understand.*
I don't know what any of it means.
Once, in another museum, you asked me to tell you
a story about the painting we stood in front of.
It had thick black strokes as if composed
with crude oil. I spoke of a building collapsing into a river.
You said *None of these artists knew about sex, not really.*
We kissed in a dark exhibit like teenagers.
Months later, I asked you which poems we read
in bed that morning and I believed your answer.
One was about a man in a museum.
Forgetting is my only way to let go of cruelty.
And which janitor, sweeping around the white bodies
at night, will find the fallen sparrow? Will they be
the kind of person who has experience,
who will think nothing of tossing the bird into a bin?
I still hope he might be their first, that they pause
to fan out his feathers with rough hands.

STILL LIFE WITH WADDED PAPER TOWELS

I wonder whether familiarity will take over.
Here, we are children

who marvel at a swirl of hair in sunlight

or the sparrow's cry for coitus.
And though I've touched a body not mine,

I'm surprised by your heat, how

I can perceive this desire so easily—
we are betrayed at our most animal.

Here, nothing is not lovely. The slatted light.

The accidental blood on my thighs,
whatever I use to clean them.

We have been painted in hard lines

and I want to blur you out—a man
is most interesting where he doesn't belong.

So you play at negation, as though we need

that bruise made new again.
Someday I will hate you.

This is your way of saying: *I owe you nothing.*

III

ODE TO HYSTERIA + ANHEDONIA

One of me is a woman
with pointed teeth in love
with my own girlish cackle
let's play games in my well-
furnished sitting room
let's have a party & invite
everyone we've met
        & kiss them all

but at my worst
I'm two women or more
the room lit by my mouth
will drop into darkness
double is double too many sometimes
        I'd rather be alone—

       *

dearest other girl
waist-deep in water
I hate you for flooding
the bedroom though maybe
it was always flooded
please don't stare at my feet
        they're only bone

but at your best
let's sleep together
since my legs are your legs
& your hands are my almost-twins
sometimes I crave your mouth
more than my own—

*

together we read the stars
& decide I'm our best prey
I ask us both again
& again
   why don't we just
    drown each other

INTRICACIES

I watched you sharpen
a knife for so long it became
thin as a cat's leg. You said
it would be best for paring
a ribcage from skin & I asked
whose skin?

*

I have a habit
of walking through theaters
with a plate of raw meat.
I beg people to try the swordfish.
Only the swordfish.
It's firm
I promise & hand you
your utensils.

*

In bed, you pull me close
by the shoulders. I say things like
>*I want to possess you—*
>*I need to drag*
>*my lips through your spine—*

In reply, you tongue my ear & whisper
fuck me please god just fuck me.

*

I only ever drink wine
when you assure me
it will taste like metal.
Let's toast. To iron.
To copper.
To the scabs we ate
as children.

*

We can never make nice.
I'm always prying open mouths
& you order me to close them.
Cradling your own hangnails,
you dream of sucking a girl's hand.
It will taste of kerosene.

*

When my house caught fire,
you laughed at my arsonist guesses.
It was me this time. Screw
your piano
you told me. It lay hunched in ash.
But I picked up an intact key & said
think of all the wolves
I can carve now.
Imagine all their new grins.

ALTERNATE REALITIES

If my meds expired.
If there were sheets for the pull-out sofa.
If I explained more fully
      how we would ruin one another.
If I'd known. If we kept the dark.
If I never woke him.
If the birds were mute
      or they'd simply said *stop it*.
If we role-played. I could have been
      the man wringing a rabbit's neck.
If my hands were naked.
If he said *there's a hole in my stomach*
      that needs a patch.
If I reminded him we all have one
      but learned to feed it coins.
If the doll I hid under his bed were my twin.
If his favorite words weren't *regrettably,*
      anchored, & breasts.
If I memorized his teeth.
If we didn't say *you remind me of* &
      I found this animal for you.
If it had been winter.
If he let me lie in his bed until he left
      & then promised
           I could come with him.

ON THE DUALITY OF

This is two rooms on opposite sides of a house.
These rooms are made for me.

One is covered in ivy: my new backbone.
One is so empty it sighs.

This is the shakes, or the white sheet
I examine for blood.

I am coated in nothing, a woman
crawling. This is my shaking:

yes. Or, this is a shaking: *need*.
I cannot help but see a rift

between ridged fingertips
and how soft a woman can be. How she

is a curve I can never reconcile.
I still smell her. Hello,

heart-racer. Hello, re-thinker. Every flower
that's red or white

dies quickly in my vase.
They beg for light even as I

am compelled to crush
each dried petal in my fist.

BIPOLAR AND ITS RELATED DISORDERS

"Do you wish to disclose any disabilities?"

II is my box—I lie in it
ten years too late.

I prefer not to answer
but at a party, I tell a girl

about my new milligrams and she says
me too. And suddenly, all I want

is to graze my thumb across her waist
or lip, but both of our lovers

watch from a backlit doorway.
Then I can mentally make

a tick: *risky sexual behavior,
self-destructive tendencies,*

barreling toward a mixed state.
She's a Gemini too.

I'll spend your life searching for
her kind of likeness, to put my palm

against that mirror and chant
with my reflection:

me too me too me too—

EROSION

Intimacy was

      the first splitting trunk

           of a fir wave, leaving

   leeward trees exposed

to winter's angry hand.

    A gap yawning

        in the wake of death.

    Someday, some young thing

will peer up, green & ready,

   from the dirt. But not for years

       & years. A new bough

   might bend to gusts, or

curl in flames. Whichever force

    comes first. I am learning how

        to forget your face.

ELEGY ENDING ON THE OCEAN FLOOR

Grief is the hand braiding and unbraiding my insides.
For months, I've tried to grasp at time: moment
of a covert kiss; low howl in my belly

at the sight of you between my thighs.
The impossibility of the thing does not stop me demanding it.
I told you time moves faster further from gravity's center

and you didn't believe me. You do not love like an albatross.
Not like a Midwest town's single intersection. To be fair,
neither do I. Regret is my heart's only tourbillon.

In another life, I'd like to be an eddying bioluminescence
or the aurora's gleaming greeting. In this one
I lust like a metronome. Death came for us

when we opened the blinds the way I knew he would:
a bright beast peering into our minds' shadowed corners.
We had the stasis of a seabird's dive; the second hand clings

to its terrible mechanism. Still, I once tried to whisper in your ear
at a frequency that would keep you. I do not know what you heard,
only that your breathing never changed:

a whale's body sinking despite its roaring grave.

I DREAMED IN SPANISH ONCE

In the noonday sun,
bats circled *la Giralda*.
      The pulse

of their slow-beating
wings shivered down
      the carved vaults.

Your long hair shone, dark:
I heard Andalusians would look
      like you.

I touched your hair & rivers
broke off in my fingers, flooding
      the tile.

We stood alone in the cathedral
as skeletons shifted
      beneath us:

Columbus & his son
& Fernando & Alfonso
      prayed aloud

to be unlocked, to stand,
to taste just a taste of wine,
      to see the sun.

I understood their pleas,
the *por favores*, the *podrías*.
      Mendigos, I thought.

HARLOT

I.
He touches my spine
my legs clench say yes open
one hand in my mouth
the other untying knots
I will tie down his white neck

II.
He asks me to press
my knees to his throat I do
my belly becomes
an offering for his mouth
his face a twisted red mask

III.
Once he sleeps I'll steal
his genitals to carry
in my back pocket
they will keep stay pink and firm
I will bury them in spring

STAGE

Someday I'll fill a swimming pool with mayflies—stuttering, they breed just this once. I'll sit on the edge and watch them molt. Callow, like a newly corked barrel. And then: imago. My reflection can only growl back, in water or oil-slick or silver. This is an exercise in forgiveness. I dip my feet in.

EPITHALAMIUM

A mourning dove rattles her throat before the day's first call.

Early sun licks the lake's surface with white.

The whisper of finer fabrics. The whisper
        of opening blooms revealing which insects live inside.

Sloped cypress lets us pretend we gather in a wood
        rather than a chapel.

Every woman's heels will sink into soft earth.
        It will be too late to clean them for the photographs.

The dove refuses to stay and listen. She has a nest to assemble.

The lake is a white marble hall. No pealing bells.

Let us stand together. Let us sit, or pray.
        Let gold change hands.

THINGS TO DO IN THE BELLY
OF A WHALE

It's been three nights,
so cloak yourself in his innards
and wait for food to rush in.
Scoop handfuls of writhing pink krill.
Brush your hair and teeth against his baleen.
Tap in time to his circulatory system—
dance and pound your feet to its rhythm.
Do not think about your loved ones.
They will believe you drowned.
Sometimes, you will feel like drowning,
but remember: what is more pitiful
than the attempt to rise?
Mark your days with something sharp
against his purpling walls
even when he shudders at this marring.
Cover your ears when he cries
his silver love song come winter.
Don't let it remind you of your small child
who still walks from room to dark room,
calling out for no one in particular.

ODE TO LOSS

There are so many things
I'm not allowed to show you.
Imagine being the last flat stone
in a river. Then, imagine
being the man who reaches for it.

WING COVERT

I keep death in a jar.
Dried fronds, snake skulls, husk
of a cicada: these things breed
in the dark. The scrap of paper
with your name on it yellows
over time; I write more names
when I wake from the same nightmare.
A pack of dogs watches me
walk home alone—a man plays
a single note on a violin—
the jungle burns out completely
& I lie in the aftermath.
At dawn my mouth aches.
I like to think we might say
goodbye in a train station or
on a bridge. In reality
it will be less glamorous.
You are the quetzal I've snared
& I've stolen a feather &
you expect to be released.
Maybe our roles are reversed.

NOTES

"A Piece of Living Heart" takes its title from the first line of Tomaž Šalamun's poem "Metka."

"Lineage" is after Terrance Hayes's poem "Ars Poetica #789."

"Black Magic Pact" is inspired by the 1973 Japanese film *Belladonna of Sadness*.

"Love Poem: Fox" owes its title to Donika Kelly.

"Viability Study" is after Solmaz Sharif's poem "Vulnerability Study" and contains a line from Roland Barthes's *A Lover's Discourse*.

"Harlot" is inspired by the life of Sada Abe.

"Things to Do in the Belly of a Whale" is after Dan Albergotti's poem "Things to Do in the Belly of the Whale."

ACKNOWLEDGEMENTS

The author gratefully acknowledges and thanks the publications in which these poems previously appeared:

"Rotation Sequence"—*Barrow Street Review*
"La Operación"—*Birdfeast*
"Daughters I Haven't Met"—*The Boiler Journal*
"Still Life with Wadded Paper Towels"—*Copper Nickel*
"Intricacies," "Outpatient Visit Summary," "Stage"—*Cosmonauts Avenue*
"Love Poem: Fox," "Wing Covert"—*Crazyhorse*
"That Which I Consider Untamable"—*Fairy Tale Review*
"Ode to My Womb"—*Hayden's Ferry Review*
"Tasseography"—*Juked*
"Apophenia"—*Muzzle Magazine*
"Aguadilla, PR"—*Pleiades Magazine*
"Omens I Chose to Ignore"—*Poetry Northwest*
"Dueña del Bosque," "Venice Beach"—*Public Pool*
"Luna de Miel," "Wedding Day: Lake Alice on a Sunday Morning," "Ode to Hysteria + Anhedonia," "On the Duality Of,"—*Quarterly West*
"I Dreamed in Spanish Once," "Mastectomy"—*The Siren*
"Ode to Loss"—*Sixth Finch*
"Ode to Desire"—*Southeast Review*
"View from a Guest House in Calabasas"—*Sycamore Review*
"At the Museum"—*Tinderbox Poetry Journal*
"Lineage"—*Winter Tangerine Review*

Thank you to the faculty and students at the Ohio State University, especially Kathy Fagan Grandinetti, Marcus Jackson, Raena Shirali, and Megan Peak for your careful, loving hands on these poems.

Thank you, Sewanee Writers Conference, Sidney Wade, and all the folks in summer 2015.

Thank you to the students and faculty at the University of Houston—Kevin Prufer, Martha Serpas, Roberto Tejada, Hayan Charara, Erin Belieu, and francine j. harris—for your guidance. To Jennifer Chang, for an unforgettable spring, and to Aimee Nezhukumatathil, for your generous reading of my work over the years.

Thank you to the UH Center for Mexican-American Studies, Inprint Houston, Writers in the Schools, the *Gulf Coast* board, Laura Calaway, Katharine Barthelme, and Misty Matin for your support.

Thank you, Tiana Clark, for choosing this one, and to Jenny Molberg and the editorial staff at Pleiades Press for shaping this book.

Thank you, William Logan—without you, none of it happens.

Special thanks to Cait Weiss Orcutt, who has done more for my poems than I have, and to Justin Jannise, for your challenging wit, creative philosophy, and friendship.

And to Maggie Cipriano, author photographer extraordinaire, my dearest friend, closest reader, and smartest critic.

All my gratitude to my family, who believes in my writing.

And to Jošt Vrabič Koren, my heart, *ljubim te*.

ABOUT THE AUTHOR

Paige Quiñones has received awards and fellowships from the Center for Mexican-American Studies, the Academy of American Poets, and Inprint Houston. Her work has appeared in *Copper Nickel*, *Crazyhorse*, *Juked*, *Lambda Literary*, *Orion Magazine*, *Poetry Northwest*, *Quarterly West*, *Sixth Finch*, and elsewhere. She earned her MFA from the Ohio State University and is currently a PhD student in poetry at the University of Houston.

THE LENA-MILES WEVER TODD PRIZE

The editors at Pleiades Press select 10-15 finalists from among those manuscripts submitted each year. An external judge selects one winner for publication. All selections are made blind to authorship in an open competition for which any poet writing in English is eligible. Lena-Miles Wever Todd Prize for Poetry Books are distributed by Louisiana State University Press.

ABOUT LENA-MILES WEVER TODD

Lena-Miles Wever Todd (1910-2000), for whom this prize is named, was a 1931 graduate of Winthrop College, where she was a Marshal and editor of *The Johnsonian*, the college newspaper. She was a lifelong poet, whose work was anthologized and privately published. She lived most of her life in Greenville, South Carolina, where she and her husband, Leonard M. Todd, supported and led numerous cultural organizations. She was also a painter. Her paintings are now in the collection of the Greenville County Museum of Art. Her family and friends created this prize in her honor.

ALSO AVAILABLE FROM PLEIADES PRESS

The Cipher by Molly Brodak
Geographic Tongue by Rodney Gomez
dark // thing by Ashley M. Jones
The Olive Trees' Jazz and Other Poems by Samira Negrouche, translated by Marilyn Hacker
Louder Birds by Angela Voras-Hills
Miracles Come on Mondays by Penelope Cray
The Imaginary Age by Leanna Petronella
Fluid States by Heidi Czerwiec
A Lesser Love by E. J. Koh
Destruction of the Lover by Luis Panini, translated by Lawrence Schimel
How to Tell if You are Human: Diagram Poems by Jessy Randall
Bridled by Amy Meng
30 Questions People Don't Ask: The Selected Poems of Inga Gaile, translated by Ieva Lešinka
The Darkness Call by Gary Fincke
In Between: Poetry Comics by Mita Mahato
Novena by Jacques J. Rancourt
Book of No Ledge: Visual Poems by Nance Van Winckel
Landscape with Headless Mama by Jennifer Ghivan
Random Exorcisms by Adrian C. Louis
Poetry Comics from the Book of Hours by Bianca Stone
The Belle Mar by Katie Bickham
Syph by Abigail Cloud
The Glacier's Wake by Katy Didden
Paradise, Indiana by Bruce Snider